50 Healthy Lunchbox Ideas for Kids Recipes for Home

By: Kelly Johnson

Table of Contents

- Turkey and Cheese Roll-Ups
- Veggie Packed Quesadillas
- Fruit Kabobs with Yogurt Dip
- Mini Caprese Skewers
- Chicken Salad Lettuce Wraps
- Hummus and Veggie Wrap
- Whole Grain Pita Pockets with Tuna Salad
- Ants on a Log (Celery with Peanut Butter and Raisins)
- Greek Yogurt Parfait with Berries
- Quinoa Salad with Cherry Tomatoes and Cucumber
- Apple Slices with Almond Butter
- Egg Salad Sandwich on Whole Wheat Bread
- Trail Mix with Nuts and Dried Fruits
- Mini Cheese and Whole Grain Crackers
- Chicken and Vegetable Stir-Fry
- Baked Sweet Potato Fries
- Cheese and Turkey Mini Muffins
- Rainbow Fruit Salad
- Cucumber and Cream Cheese Sandwiches
- Grilled Chicken Skewers
- Tomato Basil Mozzarella Skewers
- Whole Wheat Pasta Salad with Pesto
- Hard-Boiled Eggs
- Cherry Tomatoes with Balsamic Glaze
- Almond Butter and Banana Sandwich
- Veggie Chips (Sweet Potato, Zucchini, or Kale)
- Pineapple and Cottage Cheese Cups
- Turkey and Avocado Wrap
- Greek Yogurt with Honey and Granola
- Carrot and Hummus Cups
- Chicken and Cheese Quesadilla
- Whole Grain English Muffin Pizzas
- Spinach and Feta Muffins
- Watermelon Cubes
- Edamame Pods

- Whole Wheat Pita Bread with Tzatziki
- Brown Rice Sushi Rolls
- Cheese Cubes with Grapes
- Broccoli and Cheese Bites
- Mango Slices
- Cottage Cheese with Pineapple Chunks
- Spinach and Turkey Pinwheels
- Almond and Cranberry Energy Bites
- Avocado and Tomato Sandwich
- Chicken and Veggie Spring Rolls
- Berry Smoothie with Spinach
- Whole Wheat Bagel with Cream Cheese
- Mini Turkey Meatballs
- Pumpkin Seeds (Pepitas)
- Roasted Chickpeas

Turkey and Cheese Roll-Ups

Ingredients:

- Sliced turkey breast (nitrate-free)
- Cheese slices (cheddar, Swiss, or your choice)
- Whole grain or spinach tortillas
- Mustard or mayonnaise (optional)
- Lettuce leaves (optional)

Instructions:

Lay out a whole grain or spinach tortilla on a clean surface.
Place 2-3 slices of turkey evenly over the tortilla.
Add a layer of cheese slices on top of the turkey.
If desired, spread a thin layer of mustard or mayonnaise on the cheese.
Optional: Place a lettuce leaf over the cheese for added freshness.
Starting from one end, tightly roll up the tortilla with the turkey, cheese, and other ingredients inside.
Once rolled, slice the roll-up into bite-sized pieces or leave it whole for a larger wrap.
Secure the roll-ups with toothpicks if needed.

Note: These Turkey and Cheese Roll-Ups are versatile, allowing for customization based on personal preferences. Feel free to add veggies like cucumber or bell peppers for added crunch and nutrition. Pack in a lunchbox with some fresh fruit and a small container of Greek yogurt for a well-rounded and satisfying meal.

Veggie Packed Quesadillas

Ingredients:

- Whole wheat or corn tortillas
- Shredded cheese (cheddar, Monterey Jack, or a blend)
- Bell peppers, thinly sliced
- Red onion, thinly sliced
- Cherry tomatoes, halved
- Spinach leaves
- Avocado, sliced
- Olive oil
- Salsa and Greek yogurt (for dipping, optional)

Instructions:

In a skillet, heat a small amount of olive oil over medium heat.
Add the sliced bell peppers and red onion to the skillet. Sauté until they are softened and slightly caramelized.
Add cherry tomatoes to the skillet and cook for an additional 1-2 minutes until they are just softened.
Remove the vegetables from the skillet and set them aside.
Place a tortilla in the skillet. Sprinkle a generous amount of shredded cheese over one half of the tortilla.
Add a layer of sautéed vegetables, a handful of spinach leaves, and slices of avocado over the cheese.
Fold the other half of the tortilla over the filling, creating a half-moon shape.
Press the quesadilla down gently with a spatula and cook until the bottom is golden brown.
Carefully flip the quesadilla and cook the other side until it's crispy and the cheese is melted.
Remove from the skillet and let it cool for a minute before slicing into wedges.
Repeat the process for additional quesadillas.

Note: Serve these Veggie-Packed Quesadillas with salsa and Greek yogurt on the side for dipping. These quesadillas are perfect for a quick and nutritious lunch, and you can customize the veggies based on your preferences.

Fruit Kabobs with Yogurt Dip

Ingredients:

For Fruit Kabobs:

- Strawberries, hulled
- Pineapple chunks
- Grapes (red or green)
- Kiwi, peeled and sliced
- Blueberries

For Yogurt Dip:

- 1 cup Greek yogurt
- 2 tablespoons honey or maple syrup
- 1 teaspoon vanilla extract

Instructions:

For Fruit Kabobs:

Prepare all the fruits by washing and cutting them into bite-sized pieces.
Thread the fruit pieces onto wooden skewers, alternating between different fruits to create colorful kabobs.

For Yogurt Dip:

In a small bowl, mix together Greek yogurt, honey or maple syrup, and vanilla extract until well combined.
Taste the dip and adjust the sweetness if needed by adding more honey or maple syrup.

Assembly:

Arrange the fruit kabobs on a serving platter.

Serve the fruit kabobs with the yogurt dip on the side or drizzle the dip over the kabobs for added sweetness.
Optionally, chill the yogurt dip in the refrigerator for a refreshing contrast.

Note: These Fruit Kabobs with Yogurt Dip are a fun and healthy snack or dessert option.

The combination of vibrant fruits and creamy yogurt dip makes for a delightful treat.

Feel free to customize the fruit selection based on what's in season or your personal preferences. Perfect for parties, picnics, or a sweet addition to your lunchbox.

Mini Caprese Skewers

Ingredients:

- Cherry tomatoes
- Fresh mozzarella balls (bocconcini)
- Fresh basil leaves
- Balsamic glaze (store-bought or homemade)
- Toothpicks or small skewers

Instructions:

Wash the cherry tomatoes and fresh basil leaves.
Drain the fresh mozzarella balls if they are stored in liquid.
Take a toothpick or a small skewer and thread a cherry tomato, followed by a fresh basil leaf, and then a mozzarella ball.
Repeat the process for the desired number of skewers.
Arrange the Mini Caprese Skewers on a serving platter.
Just before serving, drizzle balsamic glaze over the skewers for a flavorful finish.

Note: These Mini Caprese Skewers are a delightful and elegant appetizer or snack. The combination of sweet cherry tomatoes, creamy mozzarella, and fragrant basil creates a burst of flavors in each bite. The balsamic glaze adds a touch of sweetness and acidity to enhance the overall taste. These skewers are not only visually appealing but also easy to assemble, making them a perfect addition to any gathering or as a light accompaniment to your lunchbox.

Chicken Salad Lettuce Wraps

Ingredients:

For Chicken Salad:

- 2 cups cooked chicken, shredded (rotisserie chicken works well)
- 1/2 cup celery, finely chopped
- 1/4 cup red onion, finely chopped
- 1/2 cup grapes, halved
- 1/4 cup slivered almonds
- 1/3 cup mayonnaise
- 1 tablespoon Dijon mustard
- Salt and pepper to taste

For Lettuce Wraps:

- Large lettuce leaves (such as iceberg or butter lettuce)
- Avocado slices (optional, for topping)
- Fresh herbs (such as parsley or dill, for garnish)

Instructions:

For Chicken Salad:

In a large bowl, combine shredded chicken, chopped celery, red onion, halved grapes, and slivered almonds.
In a small bowl, mix together mayonnaise and Dijon mustard until well combined.
Pour the mayonnaise mixture over the chicken mixture and toss until everything is evenly coated.
Season the chicken salad with salt and pepper to taste.

For Lettuce Wraps:

Wash and separate large lettuce leaves, ensuring they are dry.
Spoon a generous portion of the chicken salad onto each lettuce leaf.
If desired, top each wrap with avocado slices for added creaminess.

Garnish with fresh herbs for a burst of flavor.
Secure the wraps with toothpicks if needed.

Note: These Chicken Salad Lettuce Wraps are a light and refreshing option for a quick lunch or appetizer. The combination of tender chicken, crunchy celery, sweet grapes, and creamy dressing is delightful. Serving them in lettuce wraps adds a crisp and low-carb element to the dish. Customize the salad with your favorite herbs and enjoy these wraps for a healthy and satisfying meal.

Hummus and Veggie Wrap

Ingredients:

- Whole wheat or spinach tortillas
- Hummus (store-bought or homemade)
- Bell peppers, thinly sliced (assorted colors)
- Cucumber, thinly sliced
- Carrots, julienned or shredded
- Cherry tomatoes, halved
- Red onion, thinly sliced
- Fresh spinach or lettuce leaves
- Feta cheese, crumbled (optional)
- Olive oil and balsamic vinegar (for drizzling, optional)
- Salt and pepper to taste

Instructions:

Lay out a whole wheat or spinach tortilla on a clean surface.
Spread a generous layer of hummus evenly over the entire surface of the tortilla.
Arrange a layer of fresh spinach or lettuce leaves on top of the hummus.
Place slices of bell peppers, cucumber, julienned carrots, cherry tomatoes, and red onion over the greens.
If desired, crumble feta cheese over the veggies for added creaminess.
Drizzle olive oil and balsamic vinegar over the veggies for extra flavor (optional).
Season with salt and pepper to taste.
Carefully fold the sides of the tortilla and then roll it up tightly from the bottom to create a wrap.
Cut the wrap in half diagonally for easy serving.

Note: This Hummus and Veggie Wrap is a nutritious and flavorful option for a quick lunch or snack. The combination of creamy hummus and a variety of fresh, colorful vegetables makes it both satisfying and visually appealing. Feel free to customize the wrap with your favorite veggies or add a protein source like grilled chicken for an extra boost. It's a versatile and portable option for a delicious and wholesome meal.

Whole Grain Pita Pockets with Tuna Salad

Ingredients:

For Tuna Salad:

- 2 cans (5 ounces each) tuna, drained
- 1/4 cup red onion, finely chopped
- 1/4 cup celery, finely chopped
- 1/4 cup pickles or relish, chopped
- 1/3 cup mayonnaise
- 1 tablespoon Dijon mustard
- Salt and pepper to taste

For Assembly:

- Whole grain pita pockets
- Lettuce leaves
- Tomato slices
- Cucumber slices
- Avocado slices (optional)

Instructions:

For Tuna Salad:

In a bowl, combine drained tuna, finely chopped red onion, celery, pickles or relish, mayonnaise, and Dijon mustard.
Mix everything together until well combined.
Season the tuna salad with salt and pepper to taste.

For Assembly:

Cut whole grain pita pockets in half to form pockets.
Line the inside of each pita pocket with lettuce leaves.
Spoon a generous portion of tuna salad into each pita pocket.
Add tomato slices, cucumber slices, and avocado slices (if using) to the pocket.

Close the pita pocket gently.

Note: These Whole Grain Pita Pockets with Tuna Salad are a wholesome and protein-packed option for a satisfying lunch. The tuna salad is filled with crunchy vegetables and a flavorful dressing. Stuffing it into whole grain pita pockets adds fiber and makes it a convenient and portable meal. Customize the ingredients based on your preferences and enjoy this nutritious and delicious lunch option.

Ants on a Log (Celery with Peanut Butter and Raisins)

Ingredients:

- Celery stalks, washed and cut into manageable lengths
- Peanut butter (smooth or crunchy)
- Raisins

Instructions:

Spread a generous amount of peanut butter into the groove of each celery stalk. Place raisins on top of the peanut butter, creating a line of "ants" on the "log." Repeat the process for the desired number of Ants on a Log.

Note: Ants on a Log is a classic and fun snack that's perfect for kids and adults alike. The combination of crunchy celery, creamy peanut butter, and sweet raisins provides a satisfying mix of textures and flavors. It's a playful and nutritious option for a quick bite or a delightful addition to lunchboxes. Feel free to get creative and use other toppings like chocolate chips, sunflower seeds, or dried cranberries for a personalized twist.

Greek Yogurt Parfait with Berries

Ingredients:

- Greek yogurt (unsweetened)
- Mixed berries (strawberries, blueberries, raspberries)
- Granola (homemade or store-bought)
- Honey or maple syrup (optional, for drizzling)
- Chia seeds or nuts (optional, for added crunch)

Instructions:

In a glass or a bowl, start with a layer of Greek yogurt.
Add a layer of mixed berries on top of the yogurt.
Sprinkle a generous layer of granola over the berries.
Repeat the layers until you reach the top of the glass or bowl.
If desired, drizzle honey or maple syrup over the top for added sweetness.
Optional: Sprinkle chia seeds or nuts for an extra crunch.
Repeat the process for additional parfaits.

Note: This Greek Yogurt Parfait with Berries is a delightful and nutritious treat. The creamy Greek yogurt pairs perfectly with the sweet and tart flavors of fresh berries, while the granola adds a satisfying crunch. It's a versatile and customizable snack or breakfast option that can be tailored to individual preferences. Experiment with different berries, granola varieties, and toppings to create your perfect parfait.

Quinoa Salad with Cherry Tomatoes and Cucumber

Ingredients:

- 1 cup quinoa, rinsed and cooked according to package instructions
- 1 cup cherry tomatoes, halved
- 1 cucumber, diced
- 1/4 cup red onion, finely chopped
- 1/4 cup fresh parsley, chopped
- 1/4 cup feta cheese, crumbled (optional)
- 2 tablespoons olive oil
- 1 tablespoon lemon juice
- Salt and pepper to taste

Instructions:

Cook quinoa according to package instructions, then let it cool to room temperature.
In a large bowl, combine the cooked quinoa, cherry tomatoes, diced cucumber, chopped red onion, and fresh parsley.
In a small bowl, whisk together olive oil and lemon juice to create the dressing.
Pour the dressing over the quinoa mixture and toss until everything is well coated.
If using, sprinkle crumbled feta cheese over the salad.
Season with salt and pepper to taste and toss again.
Refrigerate for at least 30 minutes before serving to allow the flavors to meld.

Note: This Quinoa Salad with Cherry Tomatoes and Cucumber is a light and refreshing option for a nutritious lunch or side dish. The combination of quinoa, fresh vegetables, and a zesty dressing creates a wholesome and flavorful salad. Feel free to customize the salad by adding ingredients like olives, avocado, or grilled chicken for added protein. Enjoy it chilled on its own or as a side dish to complement your lunchbox.

Apple Slices with Almond Butter

Ingredients:

- Apples (your favorite variety), sliced
- Almond butter (or your preferred nut butter)
- Honey (optional, for drizzling)
- Cinnamon (optional, for sprinkling)

Instructions:

Wash and slice your favorite apples into thin wedges or rounds.
Spread a layer of almond butter on each apple slice.
Optionally, drizzle honey over the almond butter for added sweetness.
If desired, sprinkle a pinch of cinnamon over the top.
Arrange the apple slices on a plate or in a lunchbox for a delightful snack.

Note: Apple Slices with Almond Butter is a simple and wholesome snack that combines the crispness of fresh apples with the creaminess of almond butter. It's a satisfying and nutritious option that provides a balance of natural sugars and healthy fats. Customize the snack by experimenting with different nut butters or adding toppings like chia seeds or granola for extra texture. Enjoy this easy and delicious treat for a quick energy boost or a sweet addition to your lunchbox.

Egg Salad Sandwich on Whole Wheat Bread

Ingredients:

For Egg Salad:

- 4 hard-boiled eggs, peeled and chopped
- 1/4 cup mayonnaise
- 1 teaspoon Dijon mustard
- 1/4 cup celery, finely chopped
- 2 tablespoons red onion, finely chopped
- Salt and pepper to taste
- Fresh chives or parsley, chopped (optional, for garnish)

For Sandwich:

- Whole wheat bread slices
- Lettuce leaves
- Tomato slices
- Avocado slices (optional)

Instructions:

For Egg Salad:

In a bowl, combine the chopped hard-boiled eggs, mayonnaise, Dijon mustard, chopped celery, and chopped red onion.
Mix everything until well combined.
Season the egg salad with salt and pepper to taste.
Optionally, sprinkle fresh chives or parsley over the top for garnish.

For Sandwich:

Toast the whole wheat bread slices if desired.
Place a lettuce leaf on one slice of bread.
Spoon a generous portion of the egg salad over the lettuce.
Add tomato slices and avocado slices (if using).

Top with another slice of whole wheat bread to create a sandwich.
Repeat the process for additional sandwiches.
Cut the sandwiches in half diagonally for serving.

Note: This Egg Salad Sandwich on Whole Wheat Bread is a classic and satisfying option for lunch. The creamy egg salad pairs well with the nuttiness of whole wheat bread, and the addition of fresh vegetables adds crunch and flavor. It's a versatile recipe that can be customized to your liking—try adding mustard, pickles, or a dash of paprika for extra flair. Enjoy this wholesome and delicious sandwich as a filling lunchbox option or a quick and easy meal.

Trail Mix with Nuts and Dried Fruits

Ingredients:

- Almonds, raw or roasted
- Walnuts, raw or roasted
- Cashews, raw or roasted
- Pistachios, raw or roasted
- Dried cranberries
- Raisins
- Dried apricots, chopped
- Dark chocolate chips or chunks

Instructions:

In a mixing bowl, combine the desired quantities of almonds, walnuts, cashews, pistachios, dried cranberries, raisins, dried apricots, and dark chocolate chips or chunks.
Toss the ingredients together until well combined.

Note: Trail Mix with Nuts and Dried Fruits is a versatile and energy-packed snack that can be easily customized to suit your taste preferences. The combination of nuts provides healthy fats and protein, while the dried fruits add natural sweetness. Dark chocolate chips or chunks offer a delicious touch of indulgence. Pack this trail mix in a small container for a convenient and satisfying on-the-go snack. Adjust the ratios of nuts and dried fruits to your liking, and feel free to experiment with other ingredients like pumpkin seeds, coconut flakes, or dried mango for variety. Enjoy this wholesome and portable snack anytime you need a quick boost of energy.

Mini Cheese and Whole Grain Crackers

Ingredients:

- Mini whole grain crackers
- Cheese cubes (cheddar, gouda, or your choice)

Instructions:

Place mini whole grain crackers on a serving plate or in a small container.
Cube your preferred type of cheese into bite-sized pieces.
Arrange the cheese cubes alongside the mini crackers.

Note: Mini Cheese and Whole Grain Crackers make for a simple yet satisfying snack that combines the wholesome goodness of whole grain crackers with the rich flavor of cheese. This convenient and portable snack is perfect for a quick pick-me-up or as part of a cheese platter. Choose your favorite types of cheese to cater to your taste preferences. Pack them in a small container for an easy-to-carry snack that's ideal for a lunchbox, picnic, or a delicious treat at any time of the day.

Chicken and Vegetable Stir-Fry

Ingredients:

For Stir-Fry Sauce:

- 1/4 cup soy sauce
- 2 tablespoons oyster sauce
- 1 tablespoon hoisin sauce
- 1 tablespoon cornstarch
- 1 tablespoon water

For Stir-Fry:

- 1 pound boneless, skinless chicken breast, thinly sliced
- 2 tablespoons vegetable oil
- 3 cups mixed vegetables (broccoli florets, bell peppers, snap peas, carrots, etc.)
- 2 cloves garlic, minced
- 1 tablespoon ginger, grated
- Cooked brown rice or quinoa for serving

Instructions:

For Stir-Fry Sauce:

In a small bowl, whisk together soy sauce, oyster sauce, hoisin sauce, cornstarch, and water. Set aside.

For Stir-Fry:

Heat vegetable oil in a wok or large skillet over medium-high heat.
Add sliced chicken and stir-fry until cooked through and slightly browned.
Remove chicken from the wok and set aside.
In the same wok, add a bit more oil if needed. Stir-fry mixed vegetables until they are crisp-tender.
Add minced garlic and grated ginger to the vegetables, stirring continuously for about 30 seconds until fragrant.

Return the cooked chicken to the wok with the vegetables.
Pour the stir-fry sauce over the chicken and vegetables, tossing to coat evenly.
Cook for an additional 2-3 minutes until the sauce thickens.
Serve the chicken and vegetable stir-fry over cooked brown rice or quinoa.

Note: This Chicken and Vegetable Stir-Fry is a quick and nutritious option for a flavorful lunch or dinner. The colorful mix of vegetables and tender chicken is coated in a savory stir-fry sauce, creating a well-balanced and satisfying meal. Feel free to customize the vegetables based on your preferences, and serve it over your choice of whole grains for added fiber. This versatile stir-fry is not only delicious but also an excellent way to incorporate a variety of veggies into your lunchbox or weeknight meal.

Baked Sweet Potato Fries

Ingredients:

- 2 large sweet potatoes, peeled and cut into thin strips
- 2 tablespoons olive oil
- 1 teaspoon paprika
- 1/2 teaspoon garlic powder
- 1/2 teaspoon onion powder
- 1/2 teaspoon cumin
- Salt and pepper to taste
- Fresh parsley, chopped (optional, for garnish)

Instructions:

Preheat the oven to 425°F (220°C) and line a baking sheet with parchment paper.
In a large bowl, toss the sweet potato strips with olive oil, paprika, garlic powder, onion powder, cumin, salt, and pepper. Ensure the sweet potato strips are evenly coated.
Spread the sweet potato strips in a single layer on the prepared baking sheet, making sure they are not overcrowded.
Bake in the preheated oven for 20-25 minutes, flipping the fries halfway through, or until the fries are golden brown and crispy.
Remove from the oven and let them cool slightly.
Garnish with fresh chopped parsley if desired.
Serve the baked sweet potato fries with your favorite dipping sauce.

Note: These Baked Sweet Potato Fries are a healthier alternative to traditional fries and make a delicious side dish or snack. The spices add a flavorful kick, and the baking method ensures a crispy texture without deep frying. Pair them with your favorite dipping sauce, such as ketchup, aioli, or a yogurt-based dip. These fries are not only tasty but also packed with nutrients, making them a great addition to your lunchbox or as a tasty side for any meal.

Cheese and Turkey Mini Muffins

Ingredients:

- 1 cup all-purpose flour
- 1 teaspoon baking powder
- 1/2 teaspoon baking soda
- 1/4 teaspoon salt
- 1/2 cup unsalted butter, melted
- 1/2 cup milk
- 1 large egg
- 1 cup cooked turkey breast, diced
- 1 cup sharp cheddar cheese, shredded
- 1/4 cup green onions, finely chopped
- Salt and pepper to taste

Instructions:

Preheat the oven to 375°F (190°C) and grease a mini muffin tin or line it with mini muffin liners.
In a large bowl, whisk together the flour, baking powder, baking soda, and salt.
In a separate bowl, whisk together the melted butter, milk, and egg.
Pour the wet ingredients into the dry ingredients and stir until just combined.
Gently fold in the diced turkey, shredded cheddar cheese, and chopped green onions. Season with salt and pepper to taste.
Spoon the batter into the mini muffin cups, filling each about two-thirds full.
Bake in the preheated oven for 12-15 minutes or until the tops are golden brown and a toothpick inserted into the center comes out clean.
Allow the mini muffins to cool in the tin for a few minutes before transferring them to a wire rack to cool completely.
Serve the Cheese and Turkey Mini Muffins as a delightful appetizer or pack them in your lunchbox for a tasty snack.

Note: These Cheese and Turkey Mini Muffins are a savory and portable treat that combines the flavors of turkey and cheddar cheese in a bite-sized form. Perfect for gatherings or a quick snack, these muffins are easy to make and customizable. You can also add herbs like thyme or rosemary for extra flavor. Enjoy them warm or at room temperature, and feel free to dip them in your favorite sauce or condiment.

Rainbow Fruit Salad

Ingredients:

- Strawberries, hulled and sliced
- Oranges, peeled and segmented
- Pineapple, diced
- Kiwi, peeled and sliced
- Blueberries
- Grapes, halved
- Raspberries
- Honey or maple syrup (optional, for drizzling)
- Fresh mint leaves, chopped (optional, for garnish)

Instructions:

In a large bowl, combine the sliced strawberries, segmented oranges, diced pineapple, sliced kiwi, blueberries, halved grapes, and raspberries.
Gently toss the fruits together until well combined.
Optionally, drizzle honey or maple syrup over the fruit salad for added sweetness.
Garnish with chopped fresh mint leaves for a burst of flavor.
Serve the Rainbow Fruit Salad immediately or refrigerate for a short time to let the flavors meld.

Note: This Rainbow Fruit Salad is a vibrant and refreshing dish that celebrates the natural sweetness of a variety of fruits. The combination of different colors and flavors creates a visually appealing and nutritious treat. Drizzling honey or maple syrup enhances the sweetness, while fresh mint leaves add a delightful touch. Whether enjoyed as a snack, side dish, or dessert, this fruit salad is a perfect addition to your lunchbox or any gathering.

Cucumber and Cream Cheese Sandwiches

Ingredients:

- Thinly sliced cucumbers
- Cream cheese
- Whole wheat bread or your preferred bread
- Fresh dill, chopped (optional, for garnish)
- Lemon zest (optional, for added freshness)
- Salt and pepper to taste

Instructions:

Spread a layer of cream cheese on one side of each slice of bread.
Arrange thinly sliced cucumbers evenly over the cream cheese on one slice of bread.
Optionally, sprinkle fresh dill over the cucumbers for added flavor and garnish.
If desired, add a touch of lemon zest for a refreshing twist.
Season with salt and pepper to taste.
Top with the second slice of bread, cream cheese side down, to create a sandwich.
Press the sandwich gently and, if preferred, trim the crusts and cut it into halves or quarters.
Repeat the process for additional sandwiches.

Note: These Cucumber and Cream Cheese Sandwiches are a light and crisp option for a refreshing lunch or snack. The combination of cool cucumber slices and creamy cream cheese is simple yet satisfying. Customize the sandwiches by adding fresh herbs like dill or chives, and don't forget a touch of lemon zest for brightness. Enjoy these sandwiches as an elegant addition to a lunchbox, picnic, or afternoon tea.

Grilled Chicken Skewers

Ingredients:

For Marinade:

- 1.5 pounds boneless, skinless chicken breasts, cut into cubes
- 2 tablespoons olive oil
- 2 tablespoons soy sauce
- 1 tablespoon honey
- 2 cloves garlic, minced
- 1 teaspoon ground cumin
- 1 teaspoon paprika
- Salt and pepper to taste
- Wooden skewers, soaked in water for 30 minutes

For Serving:

- Lemon wedges
- Fresh parsley, chopped (optional, for garnish)

Instructions:

In a bowl, whisk together olive oil, soy sauce, honey, minced garlic, cumin, paprika, salt, and pepper to create the marinade.
Add the chicken cubes to the marinade, ensuring each piece is well coated.
Marinate in the refrigerator for at least 30 minutes to allow the flavors to meld.
Preheat the grill to medium-high heat.
Thread the marinated chicken cubes onto the soaked wooden skewers.
Grill the chicken skewers for 10-12 minutes, turning occasionally, until the chicken is fully cooked and has a nice char.
Remove the skewers from the grill and let them rest for a few minutes.
Serve the grilled chicken skewers with lemon wedges on the side for squeezing over the chicken.
Optionally, garnish with fresh chopped parsley.
Enjoy the grilled chicken skewers as a delicious main course or as part of a picnic or barbecue.

Note: These Grilled Chicken Skewers are not only easy to prepare but also packed with flavor. The marinade adds a savory and slightly sweet taste to the chicken, and grilling gives it a delightful smokiness. Serve these skewers with your favorite sides, such as a fresh salad or grilled vegetables, for a well-rounded and satisfying meal.

Tomato Basil Mozzarella Skewers

Ingredients:

- Cherry tomatoes
- Fresh mozzarella balls (bocconcini)
- Fresh basil leaves
- Balsamic glaze (store-bought or homemade)
- Wooden skewers, soaked in water for 30 minutes

Instructions:

Wash the cherry tomatoes and pat them dry.
Thread a cherry tomato onto the wooden skewer, followed by a fresh basil leaf and a mozzarella ball.
Repeat the process until the skewer is filled, leaving a little space at each end for easy handling.
Arrange the Tomato Basil Mozzarella Skewers on a serving platter.
Just before serving, drizzle balsamic glaze over the skewers for a burst of flavor.
Optionally, sprinkle a pinch of salt and pepper over the skewers.
Serve immediately as a refreshing appetizer or part of a picnic.

Note: Tomato Basil Mozzarella Skewers, also known as Caprese Skewers, are a classic and elegant appetizer that celebrates the flavors of fresh tomatoes, basil, and mozzarella. The balsamic glaze adds a touch of sweetness and acidity, enhancing the overall taste. These skewers are not only visually appealing but also easy to assemble, making them a perfect addition to any gathering, lunchbox, or as a light and delightful snack.

Whole Wheat Pasta Salad with Pesto

Ingredients:

For Pesto:

- 2 cups fresh basil leaves, packed
- 1/2 cup grated Parmesan cheese
- 1/2 cup pine nuts or walnuts
- 2 cloves garlic, minced
- 1/2 cup extra-virgin olive oil
- Salt and pepper to taste

For Pasta Salad:

- 8 ounces whole wheat pasta, cooked according to package instructions and cooled
- Cherry tomatoes, halved
- Cucumber, diced
- Red bell pepper, diced
- Kalamata olives, pitted and halved
- Feta cheese, crumbled
- Extra fresh basil leaves for garnish (optional)

Instructions:

For Pesto:

In a food processor, combine fresh basil, grated Parmesan, pine nuts or walnuts, and minced garlic.
Pulse until the ingredients are finely chopped.
With the food processor running, slowly drizzle in the olive oil until the pesto reaches your desired consistency.
Season with salt and pepper to taste. Set aside.

For Pasta Salad:

In a large bowl, combine the cooked and cooled whole wheat pasta with cherry tomatoes, diced cucumber, diced red bell pepper, Kalamata olives, and crumbled feta cheese.

Add the prepared pesto to the pasta and vegetables, tossing everything until well coated.

Garnish with extra fresh basil leaves if desired.

Refrigerate the pasta salad for at least 30 minutes to let the flavors meld.

Serve chilled and enjoy as a refreshing and wholesome meal.

Note: This Whole Wheat Pasta Salad with Pesto is a nutritious and flavorful dish that combines the goodness of whole wheat pasta with the vibrant flavors of pesto and assorted vegetables. It's a versatile recipe that can be customized with your favorite veggies and additional protein sources like grilled chicken or chickpeas. Perfect for a light lunch, picnic, or a side dish for any occasion, this pasta salad is both satisfying and delicious.

Hard-Boiled Eggs

Ingredients:

- Eggs (as many as desired)

Instructions:

Place the eggs in a single layer in a saucepan or pot.
Add enough water to the pot to cover the eggs by at least an inch.
Place the pot on the stove over medium-high heat and bring the water to a boil.
Once the water reaches a rolling boil, reduce the heat to low and let the eggs simmer for about 9-12 minutes, depending on the desired doneness.
For soft-boiled eggs with a runny yolk, cook for about 4-6 minutes. For medium-boiled eggs with a slightly runny yolk, cook for 7-9 minutes.
Once the eggs are cooked, immediately transfer them to a bowl of ice water to cool rapidly and stop the cooking process.
Let the eggs sit in the ice water for at least 5 minutes to ensure they are fully cooled.
Gently tap the eggs on a hard surface to crack the shell, then peel the shell away.
Rinse the peeled eggs under cold water to remove any remaining shell pieces.
Your hard-boiled eggs are now ready to be sliced, chopped, or enjoyed whole.

Note: Hard-boiled eggs are a versatile and protein-packed food that can be enjoyed on their own, sliced into salads, or transformed into deviled eggs. The key to easy peeling is to shock them in ice water immediately after cooking. Adjust the cooking time based on your preference for yolk consistency. These hard-boiled eggs are perfect for adding a protein boost to your salads, sandwiches, or enjoying as a snack.

Cherry Tomatoes with Balsamic Glaze

Ingredients:

- Cherry tomatoes, washed
- Balsamic glaze (store-bought or homemade)
- Fresh basil leaves, for garnish (optional)
- Salt and pepper, to taste

Instructions:

Prepare Cherry Tomatoes:
- Wash the cherry tomatoes and pat them dry.

Assemble:
- Arrange the cherry tomatoes on a serving plate or platter.

Drizzle with Balsamic Glaze:
- Drizzle balsamic glaze over the cherry tomatoes. Use as much or as little as desired.

Season:
- Sprinkle a pinch of salt and pepper over the tomatoes for added flavor.

Garnish:
- Optionally, garnish the dish with fresh basil leaves for a burst of freshness.

Serve:
- Serve the Cherry Tomatoes with Balsamic Glaze as a refreshing side dish, appetizer, or part of a salad.

Note: This simple dish of Cherry Tomatoes with Balsamic Glaze is a quick and elegant way to enjoy the sweetness of ripe cherry tomatoes. The balsamic glaze adds a tangy and slightly sweet flavor, enhancing the natural taste of the tomatoes. It's a versatile dish that can be served as a side, appetizer, or paired with fresh mozzarella for a classic Caprese-style salad. Customize it with additional herbs like basil or thyme for extra freshness.

Almond Butter and Banana Sandwich

Ingredients:

- 2 slices whole grain bread
- Almond butter (or your favorite nut butter)
- 1 ripe banana, sliced
- Honey (optional, for drizzling)
- Cinnamon (optional, for sprinkling)

Instructions:

Spread Almond Butter:
- Spread a generous layer of almond butter on one or both slices of whole grain bread.

Add Banana Slices:
- Arrange the sliced banana evenly over the almond butter on one slice of bread.

Optional Drizzle:
- If desired, drizzle honey over the banana slices for added sweetness.

Optional Sprinkle:
- Optionally, sprinkle a dash of cinnamon over the banana slices for extra flavor.

Assemble Sandwich:
- Place the second slice of bread on top to create a sandwich.

Slice and Serve:
- If desired, cut the sandwich in half diagonally for easier handling.

Enjoy:
- Indulge in the deliciousness of the Almond Butter and Banana Sandwich!

Note: This Almond Butter and Banana Sandwich is a wholesome and satisfying option for breakfast or a snack. The creamy almond butter pairs perfectly with the natural sweetness of ripe bananas, and the addition of honey and cinnamon adds extra layers of flavor. Use whole grain bread for added fiber and nutrients. This simple and delicious sandwich is not only tasty but also provides a good balance of healthy fats, protein, and carbohydrates.

Veggie Chips (Sweet Potato, Zucchini, or Kale)

Ingredients:

- Sweet potatoes, zucchinis, or kale (or a combination)
- Olive oil
- Salt and pepper, to taste
- Optional seasonings: paprika, garlic powder, onion powder, or chili powder

Instructions:

For Sweet Potato Chips:

Preheat the oven to 375°F (190°C).
Wash and peel sweet potatoes. Slice them thinly using a mandoline or a sharp knife.
In a bowl, toss sweet potato slices with olive oil, salt, pepper, and any optional seasonings.
Arrange the sweet potato slices on a baking sheet in a single layer, making sure they do not overlap.
Bake in the preheated oven for 15-20 minutes or until the edges are crisp and golden brown. Flip the chips halfway through the baking time.

For Zucchini Chips:

Preheat the oven to 425°F (220°C).
Wash and slice zucchinis into thin rounds.
In a bowl, toss zucchini slices with olive oil, salt, pepper, and any optional seasonings.
Place the zucchini slices on a baking sheet in a single layer.
Bake in the preheated oven for 10-15 minutes or until the chips are golden and crispy, flipping once during baking.

For Kale Chips:

Preheat the oven to 300°F (150°C).
Wash and thoroughly dry kale leaves. Remove the tough stems and tear the leaves into bite-sized pieces.
In a bowl, massage kale pieces with olive oil, salt, and pepper until evenly coated.
Arrange the kale pieces on a baking sheet in a single layer.

Bake in the preheated oven for 10-15 minutes or until the kale is crispy, making sure to check frequently to prevent burning.

Note: Veggie chips are a delicious and nutritious alternative to traditional potato chips. You can choose to make sweet potato, zucchini, or kale chips, or even a combination of these veggies. Experiment with different seasonings to add your favorite flavors. These chips make for a satisfying and crunchy snack that's perfect for a movie night, lunchbox addition, or a healthier alternative to store-bought chips.

Pineapple and Cottage Cheese Cups

Ingredients:

- Fresh pineapple, diced
- Cottage cheese
- Honey (optional, for drizzling)
- Mint leaves, for garnish (optional)

Instructions:

Prepare Pineapple:
- Peel and dice fresh pineapple into bite-sized pieces.

Assemble Cups:
- In serving cups or bowls, layer the diced pineapple with cottage cheese.

Optional Drizzle:
- If desired, drizzle honey over the pineapple and cottage cheese for added sweetness.

Garnish:
- Garnish the cups with fresh mint leaves for a burst of freshness.

Serve:
- Serve the Pineapple and Cottage Cheese Cups immediately as a refreshing snack or dessert.

Note: These Pineapple and Cottage Cheese Cups are a simple and delicious way to enjoy a light and healthy snack. The natural sweetness of fresh pineapple complements the creamy texture of cottage cheese. Drizzling honey adds an extra touch of sweetness, and garnishing with mint leaves enhances the overall freshness. This snack is not only tasty but also provides a good balance of protein and vitamins. Enjoy it as a quick and satisfying treat or as a delightful addition to your lunchbox.

Turkey and Avocado Wrap

Ingredients:

- Whole wheat or spinach tortilla wraps
- Turkey slices (smoked or roasted)
- Avocado, sliced
- Lettuce leaves
- Tomato, sliced
- Red onion, thinly sliced
- Mustard or mayonnaise (optional)
- Salt and pepper to taste

Instructions:

Lay the tortilla wrap on a flat surface.
Assemble the Ingredients:
- Arrange turkey slices on the tortilla, leaving a border around the edges.

Add Avocado:
- Place sliced avocado over the turkey.

Layer Lettuce, Tomato, and Onion:
- Add lettuce leaves, sliced tomato, and thinly sliced red onion on top of the avocado.

Optional Condiments:
- If desired, spread a thin layer of mustard or mayonnaise over the ingredients.

Season:
- Season with salt and pepper to taste.

Wrap It Up:
- Fold the sides of the tortilla and then roll it up tightly from the bottom to form the wrap.

Slice and Serve:
- Optionally, slice the wrap diagonally for easier handling.

Enjoy:
- Serve the Turkey and Avocado Wrap immediately and savor the delicious combination of flavors.

Note: This Turkey and Avocado Wrap is a quick and nutritious meal option, perfect for lunch or a light dinner. The combination of lean turkey, creamy avocado, and fresh vegetables creates a satisfying and well-balanced wrap. Customize it with your favorite condiments and additional veggies. It's a versatile recipe that can be easily packed for on-the-go meals or enjoyed at home.

Greek Yogurt with Honey and Granola

Ingredients:

- Greek yogurt
- Honey
- Granola
- Fresh berries (optional)

Instructions:

Scoop Greek Yogurt:
- Spoon a generous amount of Greek yogurt into a serving bowl or glass.

Drizzle with Honey:
- Drizzle honey over the Greek yogurt to your desired sweetness.

Add Granola:
- Sprinkle a generous amount of granola over the yogurt and honey.

Optional Fresh Berries:
- If desired, top the yogurt and granola with fresh berries for added flavor and color.

Serve:
- Serve the Greek Yogurt with Honey and Granola immediately as a delicious and nutritious breakfast, snack, or dessert.

Note: This Greek Yogurt with Honey and Granola is a classic and delightful combination that offers a perfect balance of creaminess, sweetness, and crunch. Greek yogurt provides protein and a creamy texture, while honey adds natural sweetness. Granola contributes a satisfying crunch and additional nutrients. Customize this dish with your favorite granola flavor and fresh berries for a burst of freshness. Enjoy it as a quick and wholesome breakfast or a satisfying snack that can be enjoyed at any time of the day.

Carrot and Hummus Cups

Ingredients:

- Carrot sticks or baby carrots
- Hummus
- Fresh parsley, chopped (optional, for garnish)

Instructions:

> Prepare Carrot Sticks:
> - Wash and peel carrots, then cut them into sticks or use pre-cut baby carrots.
>
> Fill Cups with Hummus:
> - Spoon a dollop of hummus into individual small cups or bowls.
>
> Insert Carrot Sticks:
> - Insert carrot sticks into the hummus-filled cups, arranging them in a neat and upright manner.
>
> Garnish (Optional):
> - Optionally, sprinkle chopped fresh parsley over the hummus for a touch of color and added freshness.
>
> Serve:
> - Serve the Carrot and Hummus Cups as a nutritious and flavorful snack or appetizer.

Note: Carrot and Hummus Cups are a simple and wholesome snack that combines the crispness of fresh carrots with the creamy goodness of hummus. This snack is not only delicious but also provides a satisfying crunch and a dose of nutrients. Customize it with your favorite hummus flavor or add a sprinkle of fresh herbs for extra flair. Perfect for a light lunchbox addition, party appetizer, or a quick and healthy snack.

Chicken and Cheese Quesadilla

Ingredients:

- Flour tortillas
- Cooked chicken breast, shredded or diced
- Shredded cheese (cheddar, Monterey Jack, or a blend)
- Salsa
- Sour cream
- Green onions, chopped (optional)
- Jalapeños, sliced (optional)
- Olive oil or butter for cooking

Instructions:

Prepare the Chicken:
- Ensure the chicken is cooked and shredded or diced.

Assemble the Quesadilla:
- Place one tortilla on a flat surface. Spread a layer of shredded cheese on one half of the tortilla.
- Add a portion of the cooked chicken over the cheese.
- Optionally, add chopped green onions and sliced jalapeños for extra flavor.

Top with More Cheese:
- Sprinkle another layer of shredded cheese over the chicken and toppings.

Fold the Quesadilla:
- Fold the tortilla in half, covering the side with the chicken and cheese.

Cook:
- Heat a pan over medium heat. Add a small amount of olive oil or butter.
- Place the quesadilla in the pan and cook for 2-3 minutes on each side or until the tortilla is golden brown and the cheese is melted.

Slice and Serve:
- Remove the quesadilla from the pan and let it rest for a moment before slicing it into wedges.
- Serve hot with salsa and sour cream on the side.

Enjoy:
- Enjoy your Chicken and Cheese Quesadilla as a tasty and satisfying meal.

Note: This Chicken and Cheese Quesadilla is a quick and flavorful dish that can be easily customized with your favorite ingredients. The combination of tender chicken, melted cheese, and optional toppings creates a delicious and hearty quesadilla. Serve it for lunch, dinner, or as a party snack. Adjust the level of spiciness by adding more or fewer jalapeños, and feel free to experiment with different types of cheese for added variety.

Whole Grain English Muffin Pizzas

Ingredients:

- Whole grain English muffins, split in half
- Tomato sauce or pizza sauce
- Shredded mozzarella cheese
- Your choice of pizza toppings:
    - Pepperoni slices
    - Sliced bell peppers
    - Sliced black olives
    - Sliced mushrooms
    - Cooked and crumbled sausage
    - Fresh basil leaves
    - Cherry tomatoes, sliced
- Olive oil (optional, for brushing)

Instructions:

Preheat the Oven:
- Preheat your oven to 400°F (200°C).

Prepare English Muffins:
- Split the whole grain English muffins in half, creating a total of four halves.

Assemble Pizzas:
- Place the English muffin halves on a baking sheet.
- Spread a layer of tomato sauce or pizza sauce on each English muffin half.

Add Cheese and Toppings:
- Sprinkle shredded mozzarella cheese over the sauce.
- Add your choice of pizza toppings, such as pepperoni slices, bell peppers, olives, mushrooms, sausage, basil, or cherry tomatoes.

Optional Brush with Olive Oil:
- Optionally, brush the edges of the English muffins with a little olive oil for a golden finish.

Bake:
- Bake in the preheated oven for about 10-12 minutes or until the cheese is melted and bubbly, and the edges are golden brown.

Slice and Serve:
- Remove from the oven and let the English muffin pizzas cool for a minute.
- Slice each pizza into halves or quarters.

Enjoy:
- Enjoy your delicious Whole Grain English Muffin Pizzas as a quick and customizable meal.

Note: These Whole Grain English Muffin Pizzas are a convenient and customizable option for a quick lunch or dinner. Using whole grain English muffins adds a wholesome touch to this classic favorite. Get creative with your toppings to suit your preferences. Kids and adults alike will enjoy assembling their own personalized pizzas. Serve them with a side salad for a well-rounded meal.

Spinach and Feta Muffins

Ingredients:

- 2 cups fresh spinach, chopped
- 1/2 cup feta cheese, crumbled
- 1/4 cup grated Parmesan cheese
- 1 1/2 cups all-purpose flour
- 1 tablespoon baking powder
- 1/2 teaspoon baking soda
- 1/2 teaspoon salt
- 1/4 teaspoon black pepper
- 2 large eggs
- 1 cup buttermilk
- 1/4 cup olive oil
- 1 clove garlic, minced
- Cooking spray or muffin liners

Instructions:

Preheat the Oven:
- Preheat your oven to 375°F (190°C). Grease a muffin tin or line it with muffin liners.

Prepare Spinach and Feta Mixture:
- In a bowl, combine chopped spinach, crumbled feta cheese, and grated Parmesan cheese. Set aside.

Mix Dry Ingredients:
- In a large mixing bowl, whisk together flour, baking powder, baking soda, salt, and black pepper.

Whisk Wet Ingredients:
- In another bowl, whisk together eggs, buttermilk, olive oil, and minced garlic.

Combine Wet and Dry Mixtures:
- Pour the wet ingredients into the dry ingredients and stir until just combined.

Fold in Spinach and Feta Mixture:
- Gently fold in the spinach and feta mixture into the batter until evenly distributed.

Fill Muffin Cups:

- Spoon the batter into the prepared muffin cups, filling each about two-thirds full.

Bake:
- Bake in the preheated oven for 18-20 minutes or until the tops are golden brown and a toothpick inserted into the center comes out clean.

Cool:
- Allow the muffins to cool in the tin for a few minutes before transferring them to a wire rack to cool completely.

Serve:
- Serve the Spinach and Feta Muffins warm or at room temperature.

Note: These Spinach and Feta Muffins are a savory and satisfying treat. Packed with the goodness of spinach and the richness of feta and Parmesan cheeses, they make for a delicious breakfast or snack. The garlic adds a flavorful kick, making these muffins a tasty and wholesome option. Enjoy them on their own or paired with a salad for a light meal.

Watermelon Cubes

Ingredients:

- Fresh watermelon

Instructions:

Prepare the Watermelon:
- Wash the watermelon thoroughly.

Cut into Cubes:
- Slice off both ends of the watermelon to create stable surfaces.
- Stand the watermelon on one end and use a sharp knife to carefully cut away the rind, following the contour of the fruit.
- Cut the watermelon into slices, and then into cubes by making perpendicular cuts.

Serve:
- Place the watermelon cubes in a serving bowl or arrange them on a platter.

Optional:
- Optionally, refrigerate the watermelon cubes for a refreshing, chilled snack.

Enjoy:
- Serve the Watermelon Cubes as a hydrating and delicious snack.

Note: Watermelon cubes are a simple, hydrating, and naturally sweet treat that's perfect for hot days or as a refreshing snack. You can also get creative by adding a sprinkle of mint leaves or a squeeze of lime for extra flavor. These cubes are not only delicious but also a good source of hydration and essential nutrients.

Edamame Pods

Ingredients:

- Edamame pods (fresh or frozen)
- Sea salt (optional, for seasoning)

Instructions:

Prepare Edamame Pods:
- If using fresh edamame pods, wash them thoroughly. If using frozen edamame, thaw them according to package instructions.

Steam or Boil:
- Steam or boil the edamame pods until they are tender. This usually takes about 3-5 minutes for fresh edamame and 2-3 minutes for frozen.

Drain (if Boiled):
- If boiled, drain the edamame pods.

Season (Optional):
- While the edamame pods are still warm, sprinkle them with sea salt if desired. Toss the pods to coat them evenly.

Serve:
- Place the edamame pods in a serving bowl.

To Eat:
- To eat, hold the pod by the stem end, place the other end in your mouth, and slide out the edamame beans with your teeth.

Enjoy:
- Enjoy the Edamame Pods as a nutritious and satisfying snack.

Note: Edamame pods are not only delicious but also packed with protein and essential nutrients. They make for a great appetizer or snack, and the act of popping the beans out of the pods can be a fun and interactive experience. Serve them with a sprinkle of sea salt for a simple and tasty treat. Edamame is a versatile ingredient that can also be added to salads, stir-fries, or enjoyed on its own as a wholesome snack.

Whole Wheat Pita Bread with Tzatziki

Ingredients:

- Whole wheat pita bread
- Tzatziki sauce (store-bought or homemade)

For Tzatziki Sauce:

- 1 cup Greek yogurt
- 1 cucumber, finely diced
- 2 cloves garlic, minced
- 1 tablespoon fresh dill, chopped
- 1 tablespoon fresh mint, chopped (optional)
- 1 tablespoon extra-virgin olive oil
- Salt and pepper to taste
- Lemon juice (optional, for extra freshness)

Instructions:

For Tzatziki Sauce:

In a bowl, combine Greek yogurt, finely diced cucumber, minced garlic, chopped dill, chopped mint (if using), and olive oil.
Mix the ingredients well until the tzatziki sauce is smooth.
Season with salt and pepper to taste. Add a splash of lemon juice for extra freshness if desired.
Refrigerate the tzatziki sauce for at least 30 minutes before serving to allow the flavors to meld.

For Whole Wheat Pita Bread with Tzatziki:

Warm the whole wheat pita bread in a toaster, oven, or on a skillet for a minute or two until it's pliable.
Cut the pita bread into wedges or leave it whole, depending on your preference.
Serve the warm whole wheat pita bread with a side of tzatziki sauce for dipping.

Optionally, garnish the tzatziki with a drizzle of olive oil and a sprinkle of fresh dill before serving.
Enjoy the Whole Wheat Pita Bread with Tzatziki as a delicious and wholesome appetizer or snack.

Note: This Whole Wheat Pita Bread with Tzatziki is a healthy and flavorful option inspired by Greek cuisine. The whole wheat pita adds a nutty and hearty flavor, while the tzatziki sauce provides a creamy and refreshing dip. It's perfect for serving as an appetizer, snack, or as part of a Mediterranean-inspired meal. Customize the tzatziki with your favorite herbs and spices for a personalized touch.

Brown Rice Sushi Rolls

Ingredients:

- Nori (seaweed) sheets
- Brown rice, cooked and seasoned with rice vinegar, sugar, and salt
- Assorted vegetables (carrots, cucumber, avocado, bell peppers), julienned
- Cooked and seasoned protein (cooked shrimp, crab, or smoked salmon), optional
- Soy sauce, for dipping
- Pickled ginger and wasabi, for serving

Instructions:

Prepare Brown Rice:
- Cook brown rice according to package instructions. Once cooked, season it with a mixture of rice vinegar, sugar, and salt while it's still warm. Allow the rice to cool to room temperature.

Prepare Vegetables and Protein:
- Julienne the vegetables and prepare any protein you want to include.

Assembly Station:
- Set up a clean and flat surface for rolling sushi, and have a bowl of water nearby to wet your hands and knife.

Place Nori on Bamboo Mat:
- Place a sheet of nori, shiny side down, on a bamboo sushi rolling mat.

Spread Brown Rice:
- Wet your hands to prevent the rice from sticking, then spread a thin layer of brown rice evenly over the nori, leaving about half an inch at the top edge.

Add Fillings:
- Arrange the julienned vegetables and protein along the bottom edge of the rice.

Rolling:
- Using the bamboo mat, start rolling the sushi from the bottom, applying gentle pressure. Continue rolling until you reach the exposed edge of the nori.

Seal the Edge:
- Wet the exposed edge of the nori with a bit of water to seal the roll.

Slice:

- Using a sharp knife, wet it slightly, then slice the roll into bite-sized pieces.

Serve:
- Serve the brown rice sushi rolls with soy sauce, pickled ginger, and wasabi.

Enjoy:
- Enjoy your homemade Brown Rice Sushi Rolls as a nutritious and delicious meal or snack.

Note: Brown Rice Sushi Rolls provide a healthier twist to traditional sushi by incorporating nutrient-rich brown rice. You can customize the fillings to suit your taste, making it a versatile and satisfying option. Serve with soy sauce, pickled ginger, and wasabi for a complete sushi experience at home.

Cheese Cubes with Grapes

Ingredients:

- Cheese cubes (Cheddar, Gouda, or your favorite cheese)
- Fresh grapes (red or green)

Instructions:

Prepare Cheese Cubes:
- Cut your preferred cheese into bite-sized cubes. You can use a variety of cheeses for a diverse flavor experience.

Wash Grapes:
- Wash the grapes thoroughly and pat them dry with a paper towel.

Assemble:
- Skewer a cheese cube followed by a grape onto toothpicks or small skewers. Repeat the process for the desired number of cheese and grape skewers.

Serve:
- Arrange the Cheese Cubes with Grapes skewers on a serving platter.

Enjoy:
- Enjoy this simple and elegant snack that combines the creamy richness of cheese with the sweetness of grapes.

Note: Cheese Cubes with Grapes make for a delightful and effortless appetizer or snack, offering a perfect balance of flavors and textures. The combination of creamy cheese and juicy grapes is not only delicious but also visually appealing. Serve these skewers at parties, gatherings, or enjoy them as a quick and satisfying treat. Experiment with different cheese varieties to add a creative touch to this classic pairing.

Broccoli and Cheese Bites

Ingredients:

- 2 cups broccoli florets, steamed and finely chopped
- 1 cup cheddar cheese, shredded
- 1/2 cup breadcrumbs
- 2 large eggs, beaten
- 1/4 cup grated Parmesan cheese
- 1/2 teaspoon garlic powder
- Salt and pepper to taste
- Cooking spray or olive oil for greasing

Instructions:

Preheat the Oven:
- Preheat your oven to 375°F (190°C). Grease a mini muffin tin with cooking spray or olive oil.

Combine Ingredients:
- In a large mixing bowl, combine the finely chopped steamed broccoli, cheddar cheese, breadcrumbs, beaten eggs, grated Parmesan cheese, garlic powder, salt, and pepper. Mix well until all ingredients are evenly combined.

Form Bites:
- Using a spoon, scoop the mixture and press it into each cup of the mini muffin tin, forming bite-sized portions.

Bake:
- Bake in the preheated oven for about 15-18 minutes or until the edges are golden brown and the bites are set.

Cool:
- Allow the Broccoli and Cheese Bites to cool for a few minutes in the muffin tin before transferring them to a wire rack.

Serve:
- Serve the bites warm as a delicious and nutritious appetizer or snack.

Optional Dipping Sauce:
- Prepare a dipping sauce with yogurt, sour cream, or a favorite dressing for added flavor.

Enjoy:

- Enjoy these tasty Broccoli and Cheese Bites as a healthy and satisfying option for any occasion.

Note: Broccoli and Cheese Bites are a fantastic way to incorporate vegetables into a snack or appetizer. Packed with the goodness of broccoli and the cheesy goodness of cheddar, these bites are not only delicious but also a great source of nutrients. They're perfect for parties, lunchboxes, or as an anytime snack. Feel free to customize the seasonings and serve them with your preferred dipping sauce.

Mango Slices

Ingredients:

- Ripe mangoes

Instructions:

Choose Ripe Mangoes:
- Select ripe mangoes that yield slightly to gentle pressure and have a fruity aroma near the stem.

Wash Mangoes:
- Wash the mangoes thoroughly under running water.

Peel the Mango:
- Using a knife, carefully peel the skin off the mango. You can also use a vegetable peeler or a mango peeler.

Slice:
- Hold the peeled mango upright and slice along both sides of the flat, oblong seed in the center. You should have two large slices and the seed.

Remove Flesh from Seed:
- Trim any remaining flesh from the seed and slice off any additional mango pieces.

Slice or Dice:
- Cut the mango slices into smaller pieces if desired. You can either slice them into thin strips or dice them into bite-sized cubes.

Serve:
- Arrange the mango slices on a plate or in a bowl.

Optional:
- Optionally, squeeze some lime or sprinkle a pinch of chili powder for added flavor.

Chill (Optional):
- If desired, refrigerate the mango slices for a refreshing, chilled snack.

Enjoy:
- Enjoy the Mango Slices as a juicy and delicious snack.

Note: Mango slices are a simple, refreshing, and naturally sweet snack that requires minimal preparation. Enjoy them on their own or add them to fruit salads, yogurt, or desserts. Mangoes are not only delicious but also rich in vitamins and antioxidants.

Additionally, they make a great addition to summer picnics or as a healthy treat for kids and adults alike.

Cottage Cheese with Pineapple Chunks

Ingredients:

- Cottage cheese
- Fresh pineapple chunks

Instructions:

Prepare Cottage Cheese:
- Scoop the desired amount of cottage cheese into a serving bowl.

Prepare Pineapple Chunks:
- Peel and core a fresh pineapple. Cut it into bite-sized chunks.

Combine:
- Gently fold the fresh pineapple chunks into the cottage cheese.

Serve:
- Serve the Cottage Cheese with Pineapple Chunks immediately.

Optional Variations:
- Optionally, drizzle honey or sprinkle a bit of cinnamon over the cottage cheese and pineapple for added flavor.

Chill (Optional):
- If desired, refrigerate the dish for a short time before serving for a refreshing, chilled snack.

Enjoy:
- Enjoy this simple and wholesome combination of cottage cheese and pineapple as a nutritious snack or light meal.

Note: Cottage Cheese with Pineapple Chunks is a classic and delicious pairing that combines the creamy texture of cottage cheese with the sweet and tangy flavor of fresh pineapple. It's a quick and easy snack that provides a balance of protein and natural sweetness. Customize it with your preferred cottage cheese consistency and the amount of pineapple to suit your taste. This dish can be enjoyed for breakfast, as a snack, or even as a light dessert.

Spinach and Turkey Pinwheels

Ingredients:

- Whole wheat or spinach tortillas
- Cream cheese, softened
- Turkey slices (smoked or roasted)
- Fresh spinach leaves, washed and dried
- Red bell pepper, thinly sliced (optional)
- Garlic powder (optional)
- Black pepper, to taste
- Toothpicks (optional, for securing pinwheels)

Instructions:

Prepare Tortillas:
- Lay the whole wheat or spinach tortillas on a flat surface.

Spread Cream Cheese:
- Spread a layer of softened cream cheese evenly over each tortilla.

Layer with Turkey and Spinach:
- Place turkey slices evenly over the cream cheese layer.
- Add a layer of fresh spinach leaves on top of the turkey slices.
- Optionally, add thinly sliced red bell pepper for extra crunch and flavor.

Season (Optional):
- Sprinkle a pinch of garlic powder and black pepper over the ingredients for added flavor.

Roll into Pinwheels:
- Starting from one end, tightly roll up the tortilla into a log or cylinder shape.

Slice into Pinwheels:
- Use a sharp knife to slice the rolled tortilla into individual pinwheels.

Secure with Toothpicks (Optional):
- If desired, secure the pinwheels with toothpicks to hold their shape.

Serve:
- Arrange the Spinach and Turkey Pinwheels on a plate.

Chill (Optional):
- Optionally, refrigerate the pinwheels for a short time before serving for a cool and refreshing appetizer.

Enjoy:

- Enjoy these flavorful and nutritious Spinach and Turkey Pinwheels as a snack or appetizer.

Note: Spinach and Turkey Pinwheels are a versatile and tasty snack or appetizer that combines the freshness of spinach with the savory goodness of turkey and cream cheese. They are not only delicious but also easy to make and can be customized with additional ingredients like red bell peppers or your favorite herbs. Perfect for parties, picnics, or as a quick and satisfying bite.

Almond and Cranberry Energy Bites

Ingredients:

- 1 cup rolled oats
- 1/2 cup almond butter
- 1/3 cup honey or maple syrup
- 1/2 cup chopped almonds
- 1/2 cup dried cranberries
- 1/4 cup ground flaxseed
- 1 teaspoon vanilla extract
- A pinch of salt (optional)

Instructions:

Combine Dry Ingredients:
- In a large bowl, combine rolled oats, chopped almonds, dried cranberries, and ground flaxseed.

Add Wet Ingredients:
- Add almond butter, honey (or maple syrup), and vanilla extract to the dry ingredients.

Mix Thoroughly:
- Mix the ingredients thoroughly until well combined. If the mixture is too dry, you can add a bit more almond butter or honey.

Chill the Mixture:
- Place the mixture in the refrigerator for about 15-30 minutes. Chilling makes it easier to handle and roll into bites.

Form Energy Bites:
- Once chilled, take small portions of the mixture and roll them into bite-sized balls using your hands. If the mixture is too sticky, you can wet your hands slightly.

Store:
- Place the Almond and Cranberry Energy Bites on a plate or tray and refrigerate for an additional 30 minutes to set.

Serve or Store:
- Serve the energy bites immediately, or store them in an airtight container in the refrigerator for up to a week.

Enjoy:

- Enjoy these nutritious and energy-boosting bites as a quick snack or pick-me-up throughout the day.

Note: Almond and Cranberry Energy Bites are a wholesome and convenient snack packed with the goodness of almonds, cranberries, and oats. They are easy to make, require no baking, and are customizable to suit your taste. These energy bites are perfect for on-the-go snacking, providing a balance of protein, fiber, and natural sweetness. Adjust the ingredients according to your preferences, and feel free to add extras like chia seeds or coconut flakes for added texture.

Avocado and Tomato Sandwich

Ingredients:

- Whole-grain bread slices
- Ripe avocado, sliced
- Tomato, sliced
- Salt and pepper, to taste
- Optional additions: lettuce, sprouts, red onion, or your favorite sandwich toppings
- Optional condiments: mayonnaise, mustard, or balsamic glaze

Instructions:

Toast the Bread (Optional):
- If desired, toast the whole-grain bread slices until they reach your preferred level of crispiness.

Prepare Avocado:
- Slice a ripe avocado and sprinkle a pinch of salt and pepper on the slices.

Slice Tomato:
- Slice the tomato into thin rounds.

Assemble the Sandwich:
- Lay out the slices of bread on a clean surface.
- Place avocado slices on one side of each bread slice.
- Arrange tomato slices on top of the avocado.

Add Toppings (Optional):
- If desired, add additional toppings like lettuce, sprouts, or red onion.

Season:
- Sprinkle a bit more salt and pepper to taste.

Condiments (Optional):
- Spread mayonnaise, mustard, or drizzle balsamic glaze on the other side of the bread slices.

Close the Sandwich:
- Place the condiment-covered side over the avocado and tomato side to close the sandwich.

Slice (Optional):
- If you prefer, slice the sandwich in half diagonally or straight down the middle.

Serve:

- Serve the Avocado and Tomato Sandwich immediately.

Enjoy:
- Enjoy this simple and delicious sandwich as a light and satisfying meal.

Note: The Avocado and Tomato Sandwich is a classic and nutritious choice that celebrates the flavors of fresh ingredients. The creamy avocado complements the juicy tomato, creating a delightful combination. Customize the sandwich with your favorite toppings and condiments for added variety. This versatile recipe is perfect for a quick lunch or a light dinner, providing a balance of healthy fats and vegetables.

Chicken and Veggie Spring Rolls

Ingredients:

- Rice paper spring roll wrappers
- Cooked chicken breast, shredded or thinly sliced
- Rice vermicelli noodles, cooked and cooled
- Carrots, julienned
- Cucumber, julienned
- Bell peppers (red or yellow), thinly sliced
- Lettuce leaves (romaine or iceberg), torn into small pieces
- Fresh cilantro leaves
- Fresh mint leaves
- Dipping sauce (hoisin sauce, peanut sauce, or soy sauce)

Instructions:

Prepare Ingredients:
- Ensure all the ingredients are prepared and ready for assembly.

Soak Rice Paper Wrappers:
- Fill a shallow dish with warm water. Dip one rice paper wrapper into the water, ensuring it's fully submerged for about 10-15 seconds until it becomes pliable.

Lay Out Wrapper:
- Place the soaked rice paper wrapper on a clean and flat surface.

Layer Ingredients:
- On the lower third of the wrapper, layer a small amount of shredded chicken, rice vermicelli noodles, julienned carrots, cucumber, bell peppers, lettuce, cilantro leaves, and mint leaves.

Fold Sides:
- Fold the sides of the rice paper wrapper over the ingredients.

Roll Tightly:
- Starting from the bottom, tightly roll the wrapper up, enclosing the filling.

Repeat:
- Repeat the process with the remaining ingredients.

Serve with Dipping Sauce:
- Serve the Chicken and Veggie Spring Rolls with your choice of dipping sauce – hoisin sauce, peanut sauce, or soy sauce.

Slice (Optional):
- If desired, slice the spring rolls in half diagonally before serving.

Enjoy:
- Enjoy these fresh and flavorful Chicken and Veggie Spring Rolls as a light and satisfying appetizer or meal.

Note: Chicken and Veggie Spring Rolls are a delightful and healthy option that combines the goodness of lean protein and crisp vegetables. The rice paper wrapper adds a light and chewy texture, making it a refreshing choice, especially during warmer seasons. Customize the filling with your favorite vegetables and herbs, and dip them in your preferred sauce for an extra burst of flavor. These spring rolls are great for gatherings, parties, or as a light lunch or dinner option.

Berry Smoothie with Spinach

Ingredients:

- 1 cup mixed berries (strawberries, blueberries, raspberries)
- 1 ripe banana
- 1 cup fresh spinach leaves, washed
- 1/2 cup Greek yogurt
- 1/2 cup almond milk (or any milk of your choice)
- 1 tablespoon chia seeds (optional)
- Ice cubes (optional)
- Honey or agave syrup for sweetness (optional)

Instructions:

Prepare Ingredients:
- Wash the berries and spinach thoroughly.

Combine in Blender:
- In a blender, combine the mixed berries, ripe banana, fresh spinach leaves, Greek yogurt, almond milk, and chia seeds (if using).

Blend Until Smooth:
- Blend the ingredients until smooth and well combined. If the consistency is too thick, you can add more almond milk.

Adjust Sweetness (Optional):
- Taste the smoothie and, if needed, add honey or agave syrup for sweetness. Blend again to combine.

Add Ice Cubes (Optional):
- If you prefer a colder smoothie, add a handful of ice cubes and blend until they are crushed and the smoothie is well chilled.

Serve:
- Pour the Berry Smoothie with Spinach into glasses.

Garnish (Optional):
- Garnish with a few whole berries or a sprinkle of chia seeds on top if desired.

Enjoy:
- Enjoy this refreshing and nutrient-packed Berry Smoothie with Spinach as a delicious and healthy breakfast or snack.

Note: This Berry Smoothie with Spinach is a tasty and nutritious way to incorporate leafy greens into your diet. The sweetness of the berries and banana masks the spinach flavor, making it a great option for those looking to add more greens to their smoothies. Feel free to customize the recipe by using your favorite berries, adjusting sweetness, or adding protein powder for an extra boost. It's a quick and convenient way to enjoy a burst of vitamins and antioxidants in a single glass.

Whole Wheat Bagel with Cream Cheese

Ingredients:

- 1 whole wheat bagel
- Cream cheese (plain or flavored)
- Optional toppings: sliced tomatoes, cucumber, smoked salmon, fresh herbs, or cracked black pepper

Instructions:

Slice and Toast the Bagel:
- If desired, slice the whole wheat bagel in half. Toast the bagel halves until they reach your preferred level of crispiness.

Spread Cream Cheese:
- While the bagel is still warm, spread a generous layer of cream cheese on each toasted half.

Optional Toppings:
- Customize your Whole Wheat Bagel with Cream Cheese by adding your favorite toppings. Sliced tomatoes, cucumber, smoked salmon, fresh herbs, or cracked black pepper are popular choices.

Assemble:
- Place the optional toppings on the cream cheese-covered bagel halves.

Serve:
- Serve the Whole Wheat Bagel with Cream Cheese immediately.

Enjoy:
- Enjoy this classic and satisfying breakfast or snack.

Note: A Whole Wheat Bagel with Cream Cheese is a versatile and wholesome option that can be enjoyed for breakfast, brunch, or as a quick snack. The whole wheat bagel adds nuttiness and extra fiber, while the cream cheese provides a creamy and indulgent touch. Customize it with your favorite toppings to add freshness and flavor. This simple yet delicious combination is a timeless favorite that can be easily prepared for a satisfying start to your day.

Mini Turkey Meatballs

Ingredients:

- 1 pound ground turkey (lean)
- 1/2 cup breadcrumbs
- 1/4 cup grated Parmesan cheese
- 1/4 cup milk
- 1 large egg
- 2 cloves garlic, minced
- 1 teaspoon dried oregano
- 1 teaspoon dried basil
- 1/2 teaspoon onion powder
- Salt and pepper to taste
- Olive oil (for greasing)

Instructions:

Preheat Oven:
- Preheat your oven to 375°F (190°C).

Prepare Baking Sheet:
- Grease a baking sheet with olive oil or line it with parchment paper to prevent sticking.

Mix Ingredients:
- In a large mixing bowl, combine ground turkey, breadcrumbs, grated Parmesan cheese, milk, egg, minced garlic, dried oregano, dried basil, onion powder, salt, and pepper.

Combine Thoroughly:
- Mix the ingredients thoroughly until well combined. Use your hands or a spoon to evenly distribute the seasonings.

Form Mini Meatballs:
- Take small portions of the mixture and roll them into mini meatballs, about 1 inch in diameter. Place the meatballs on the prepared baking sheet.

Bake:
- Bake the mini turkey meatballs in the preheated oven for approximately 15-20 minutes or until they are cooked through and golden brown on the outside.

Check Doneness:

- To ensure the meatballs are cooked through, you can cut one open to make sure there is no pink in the center.

Serve:
- Serve the Mini Turkey Meatballs hot as an appetizer, snack, or as part of a meal.

Optional Sauce:
- Optionally, serve the mini meatballs with your favorite dipping sauce or incorporate them into a pasta dish or as a topping for a salad.

Enjoy:
- Enjoy these flavorful Mini Turkey Meatballs as a tasty and protein-packed addition to your meals.

Note: Mini Turkey Meatballs are a versatile and lean protein option that can be served in various ways. They are perfect for appetizers, snacks, or as part of a meal. Customize the seasonings to suit your taste, and feel free to experiment with different dipping sauces. These mini meatballs are not only delicious but also a great make-ahead option for quick and convenient meals.

Pumpkin Seeds (Pepitas)

Ingredients:

- Fresh pumpkin seeds (seeds from a pumpkin)
- Olive oil
- Salt
- Optional seasonings: garlic powder, paprika, cayenne pepper, cinnamon, or your favorite spices

Instructions:

Clean and Rinse Seeds:
- Remove the seeds from the pumpkin and clean them by separating them from any pulp. Rinse the seeds under cold water.

Boil Seeds (Optional):
- If you prefer softer seeds, you can boil them in salted water for about 10 minutes. This step is optional and can enhance the texture.

Preheat Oven:
- Preheat your oven to 300°F (150°C).

Dry Seeds:
- Pat the pumpkin seeds dry with a clean kitchen towel or paper towels.

Season Seeds:
- In a bowl, toss the pumpkin seeds with olive oil and salt. Add optional seasonings of your choice, such as garlic powder, paprika, cayenne pepper, or cinnamon, depending on whether you prefer a savory or sweet flavor.

Spread on Baking Sheet:
- Spread the seasoned pumpkin seeds in a single layer on a baking sheet.

Roast in the Oven:
- Roast the pumpkin seeds in the preheated oven for about 20-30 minutes or until they are golden brown. Stir the seeds occasionally to ensure even roasting.

Check Doneness:
- To check if the seeds are done, taste one. They should be crunchy and have a golden color.

Cool:

- Allow the roasted pumpkin seeds to cool completely before storing or serving.

Serve or Store:
- Serve the Roasted Pumpkin Seeds as a snack or use them as a topping for salads, soups, or yogurt. Store any leftovers in an airtight container.

Enjoy:
- Enjoy the crunchy and flavorful Roasted Pumpkin Seeds as a nutritious and satisfying treat.

Note: Roasting pumpkin seeds is a simple and delicious way to make use of the seeds from your pumpkin. You can customize the seasonings based on your preferences, whether you enjoy a savory or sweet flavor profile. These crunchy and nutritious seeds make a great snack and can be sprinkled on various dishes to add texture and flavor.

Roasted Chickpeas

Ingredients:

- 1 can (15 ounces) chickpeas (garbanzo beans), drained and rinsed
- 1-2 tablespoons olive oil
- Salt, to taste
- Optional seasonings: paprika, cumin, garlic powder, chili powder, cayenne pepper, or your favorite spices

Instructions:

Preheat Oven:
- Preheat your oven to 400°F (200°C).

Dry Chickpeas:
- Drain and rinse the chickpeas. Pat them dry with a clean kitchen towel or paper towels.

Remove Skins (Optional):
- Optionally, you can remove the skins from the chickpeas by gently rubbing them with a towel. This step is optional but can result in a crispier texture.

Toss with Olive Oil:
- In a bowl, toss the chickpeas with olive oil until they are evenly coated. The oil helps in achieving a crispy texture.

Season Chickpeas:
- Sprinkle the chickpeas with salt and any additional seasonings you prefer. Common choices include paprika, cumin, garlic powder, chili powder, or cayenne pepper for added flavor.

Spread on Baking Sheet:
- Spread the seasoned chickpeas in a single layer on a baking sheet.

Roast in the Oven:
- Roast the chickpeas in the preheated oven for 20-30 minutes or until they are golden brown and crispy. Shake the baking sheet or stir the chickpeas halfway through the cooking time for even roasting.

Check Doneness:
- To check if the chickpeas are done, taste one. They should be crunchy and have a nutty flavor.

Cool:
- Allow the roasted chickpeas to cool for a few minutes before serving.

Serve or Store:
- Serve the Roasted Chickpeas as a crunchy snack or as a topping for salads and soups. Store any leftovers in an airtight container.

Enjoy:
- Enjoy these flavorful and nutritious Roasted Chickpeas as a delicious and satisfying alternative to traditional snacks.

Note: Roasted Chickpeas are a crunchy and protein-packed snack that can be seasoned to your liking. Whether you prefer a savory or spicy flavor, you can customize the seasonings to suit your taste. These roasted chickpeas are a great alternative to chips and make a nutritious addition to salads or as a topping for various dishes. Experiment with different spice combinations for a variety of flavors.

www.ingramcontent.com/pod-product-compliance
Lightning Source LLC
LaVergne TN
LVHW081615060526
838201LV00054B/2267